LOCATION_____DATE_____

DIRECTIONS_____

_____

_____

WATER LEVEL_____

ROD_____

TECHNIQUE:_____DRY_____NYMPH_____STREAMER

SPECIES_____( )   SPECIES_____( )

SPECIES_____( )   SPECIES_____( )

BEST FLY_____

ADDITIONAL NOTES_____

_____

LOCATION_____DATE_____

DIRECTIONS_____

_____

_____

WATER LEVEL_____

ROD_____

TECHNIQUE:_____DRY_____NYMPH_____STREAMER

SPECIES_____( )   SPECIES_____( )

SPECIES_____( )   SPECIES_____( )

BEST FLY_____

ADDITIONAL NOTES_____

_____

LOCATION_____DATE_____
DIRECTIONS_____
_____
_____
WATER LEVEL_____
ROD_____
TECHNIQUE:_____DRY_____NYMPH_____STREAMER
SPECIES_____( )   SPECIES_____( )
SPECIES_____( )   SPECIES_____( )
BEST FLY_____
ADDITIONAL NOTES_____
_____

LOCATION_____DATE_____
DIRECTIONS_____
_____
_____
WATER LEVEL_____
ROD_____
TECHNIQUE:_____DRY_____NYMPH_____STREAMER
SPECIES_____( )   SPECIES_____( )
SPECIES_____( )   SPECIES_____( )
BEST FLY_____
ADDITIONAL NOTES_____
_____

LOCATION_____DATE_____
DIRECTIONS_____
_____
_____
WATER LEVEL_____
ROD_____
TECHNIQUE:_____DRY_____NYMPH_____STREAMER
SPECIES_____( )   SPECIES_____( )
SPECIES_____( )   SPECIES_____( )
BEST FLY_____
ADDITIONAL NOTES_____
_____

LOCATION_____DATE_____
DIRECTIONS_____
_____
_____
WATER LEVEL_____
ROD_____
TECHNIQUE:_____DRY_____NYMPH_____STREAMER
SPECIES_____( )   SPECIES_____( )
SPECIES_____( )   SPECIES_____( )
BEST FLY_____
ADDITIONAL NOTES_____
_____

LOCATION_____DATE_____

DIRECTIONS_____

_____

_____

WATER LEVEL_____

ROD_____

TECHNIQUE:_____DRY_____NYMPH_____STREAMER

SPECIES_____( )   SPECIES_____( )

SPECIES_____( )   SPECIES_____( )

BEST FLY_____

ADDITIONAL NOTES_____

_____

LOCATION_____DATE_____

DIRECTIONS_____

_____

_____

WATER LEVEL_____

ROD_____

TECHNIQUE:_____DRY_____NYMPH_____STREAMER

SPECIES_____( )   SPECIES_____( )

SPECIES_____( )   SPECIES_____( )

BEST FLY_____

ADDITIONAL NOTES_____

_____

LOCATION_____DATE_____

DIRECTIONS_____

_____

_____

WATER LEVEL_____

ROD_____

TECHNIQUE:_____DRY_____NYMPH_____STREAMER

SPECIES_____( )   SPECIES_____( )

SPECIES_____( )   SPECIES_____( )

BEST FLY_____

ADDITIONAL NOTES_____

_____

LOCATION_____DATE_____

DIRECTIONS_____

_____

_____

WATER LEVEL_____

ROD_____

TECHNIQUE:_____DRY_____NYMPH_____STREAMER

SPECIES_____( )   SPECIES_____( )

SPECIES_____( )   SPECIES_____( )

BEST FLY_____

ADDITIONAL NOTES_____

_____

LOCATION_____DATE_____

DIRECTIONS_____

_____

_____

WATER LEVEL_____

ROD_____

TECHNIQUE:_____DRY_____NYMPH_____STREAMER

SPECIES_____( )   SPECIES_____( )

SPECIES_____( )   SPECIES_____( )

BEST FLY_____

ADDITIONAL NOTES_____

_____

LOCATION_____DATE_____

DIRECTIONS_____

_____

_____

WATER LEVEL_____

ROD_____

TECHNIQUE:_____DRY_____NYMPH_____STREAMER

SPECIES_____( )   SPECIES_____( )

SPECIES_____( )   SPECIES_____( )

BEST FLY_____

ADDITIONAL NOTES_____

_____

LOCATION_____DATE_____

DIRECTIONS_____

_____

_____

WATER LEVEL_____

ROD_____

TECHNIQUE:_____DRY_____NYMPH_____STREAMER

SPECIES_____( )   SPECIES_____( )

SPECIES_____( )   SPECIES_____( )

BEST FLY_____

ADDITIONAL NOTES_____

_____

LOCATION_____DATE_____

DIRECTIONS_____

_____

_____

WATER LEVEL_____

ROD_____

TECHNIQUE:_____DRY_____NYMPH_____STREAMER

SPECIES_____( )   SPECIES_____( )

SPECIES_____( )   SPECIES_____( )

BEST FLY_____

ADDITIONAL NOTES_____

_____

LOCATION_____DATE_____

DIRECTIONS_____

_____

_____

WATER LEVEL_____

ROD_____

TECHNIQUE:_____DRY_____NYMPH_____STREAMER

SPECIES_____( )   SPECIES_____( )

SPECIES_____( )   SPECIES_____( )

BEST FLY_____

ADDITIONAL NOTES_____

_____

LOCATION_____DATE_____

DIRECTIONS_____

_____

_____

WATER LEVEL_____

ROD_____

TECHNIQUE:_____DRY_____NYMPH_____STREAMER

SPECIES_____( )   SPECIES_____( )

SPECIES_____( )   SPECIES_____( )

BEST FLY_____

ADDITIONAL NOTES_____

_____

LOCATION_____DATE_____

DIRECTIONS_____

_____

_____

WATER LEVEL_____

ROD_____

TECHNIQUE:_____DRY_____NYMPH_____STREAMER

SPECIES_____( )   SPECIES_____( )

SPECIES_____( )   SPECIES_____( )

BEST FLY_____

ADDITIONAL NOTES_____

_____

LOCATION_____DATE_____

DIRECTIONS_____

_____

_____

WATER LEVEL_____

ROD_____

TECHNIQUE:_____DRY_____NYMPH_____STREAMER

SPECIES_____( )   SPECIES_____( )

SPECIES_____( )   SPECIES_____( )

BEST FLY_____

ADDITIONAL NOTES_____

_____

LOCATION_____DATE_____

DIRECTIONS_____

_____

_____

WATER LEVEL_____

ROD_____

TECHNIQUE:_____DRY_____NYMPH_____STREAMER

SPECIES_____( )   SPECIES_____( )

SPECIES_____( )   SPECIES_____( )

BEST FLY_____

ADDITIONAL NOTES_____

_____

LOCATION_____DATE_____

DIRECTIONS_____

_____

_____

WATER LEVEL_____

ROD_____

TECHNIQUE:_____DRY_____NYMPH_____STREAMER

SPECIES_____( )   SPECIES_____( )

SPECIES_____( )   SPECIES_____( )

BEST FLY_____

ADDITIONAL NOTES_____

_____

LOCATION_____DATE_____

DIRECTIONS_____

_____

_____

WATER LEVEL_____

ROD_____

TECHNIQUE:_____DRY_____NYMPH_____STREAMER

SPECIES_____( )   SPECIES_____( )

SPECIES_____( )   SPECIES_____( )

BEST FLY_____

ADDITIONAL NOTES_____

_____

LOCATION_____DATE_____

DIRECTIONS_____

_____

_____

WATER LEVEL_____

ROD_____

TECHNIQUE:_____DRY_____NYMPH_____STREAMER

SPECIES_____( )   SPECIES_____( )

SPECIES_____( )   SPECIES_____( )

BEST FLY_____

ADDITIONAL NOTES_____

_____

LOCATION_____DATE_____

DIRECTIONS_____

_____

_____

WATER LEVEL_____

ROD_____

TECHNIQUE:_____DRY_____NYMPH_____STREAMER

SPECIES_____( )   SPECIES_____( )

SPECIES_____( )   SPECIES_____( )

BEST FLY_____

ADDITIONAL NOTES_____

_____

LOCATION_____DATE_____

DIRECTIONS_____

_____

_____

WATER LEVEL_____

ROD_____

TECHNIQUE:_____DRY_____NYMPH_____STREAMER

SPECIES_____( )   SPECIES_____( )

SPECIES_____( )   SPECIES_____( )

BEST FLY_____

ADDITIONAL NOTES_____

_____

LOCATION_____DATE_____

DIRECTIONS_____

_____

_____

WATER LEVEL_____

ROD_____

TECHNIQUE:_____DRY_____NYMPH_____STREAMER

SPECIES_____( )   SPECIES_____( )

SPECIES_____( )   SPECIES_____( )

BEST FLY_____

ADDITIONAL NOTES_____

_____

LOCATION_____DATE_____

DIRECTIONS_____

_____

_____

WATER LEVEL_____

ROD_____

TECHNIQUE:_____DRY_____NYMPH_____STREAMER

SPECIES_____( )   SPECIES_____( )

SPECIES_____( )   SPECIES_____( )

BEST FLY_____

ADDITIONAL NOTES_____

_____

LOCATION_____DATE_____

DIRECTIONS_____

_____

_____

WATER LEVEL_____

ROD_____

TECHNIQUE:_____DRY_____NYMPH_____STREAMER

SPECIES_____( )   SPECIES_____( )

SPECIES_____( )   SPECIES_____( )

BEST FLY_____

ADDITIONAL NOTES_____

_____

LOCATION_____DATE_____

DIRECTIONS_____

_____

_____

WATER LEVEL_____

ROD_____

TECHNIQUE:_____DRY_____NYMPH_____STREAMER

SPECIES_____( )   SPECIES_____( )

SPECIES_____( )   SPECIES_____( )

BEST FLY_____

ADDITIONAL NOTES_____

_____

LOCATION_____DATE_____

DIRECTIONS_____

_____

_____

WATER LEVEL_____

ROD_____

TECHNIQUE:_____DRY_____NYMPH_____STREAMER

SPECIES_____( )   SPECIES_____( )

SPECIES_____( )   SPECIES_____( )

BEST FLY_____

ADDITIONAL NOTES_____

_____

LOCATION_____DATE_____

DIRECTIONS_____

_____

_____

WATER LEVEL_____

ROD_____

TECHNIQUE:_____DRY_____NYMPH_____STREAMER

SPECIES_____( )   SPECIES_____( )

SPECIES_____( )   SPECIES_____( )

BEST FLY_____

ADDITIONAL NOTES_____

_____

LOCATION_____DATE_____

DIRECTIONS_____

_____

_____

WATER LEVEL_____

ROD_____

TECHNIQUE:_____DRY_____NYMPH_____STREAMER

SPECIES_____( )   SPECIES_____( )

SPECIES_____( )   SPECIES_____( )

BEST FLY_____

ADDITIONAL NOTES_____

_____

LOCATION_____DATE_____

DIRECTIONS_____

_____

_____

WATER LEVEL_____

ROD_____

TECHNIQUE:_____DRY_____NYMPH_____STREAMER

SPECIES_____( )   SPECIES_____( )

SPECIES_____( )   SPECIES_____( )

BEST FLY_____

ADDITIONAL NOTES_____

_____

LOCATION_____DATE_____

DIRECTIONS_____

_____

_____

WATER LEVEL_____

ROD_____

TECHNIQUE:_____DRY_____NYMPH_____STREAMER

SPECIES_____( )   SPECIES_____( )

SPECIES_____( )   SPECIES_____( )

BEST FLY_____

ADDITIONAL NOTES_____

_____

LOCATION_____DATE_____

DIRECTIONS_____

_____

_____

WATER LEVEL_____

ROD_____

TECHNIQUE:_____DRY_____NYMPH_____STREAMER

SPECIES_____( )   SPECIES_____( )

SPECIES_____( )   SPECIES_____( )

BEST FLY_____

ADDITIONAL NOTES_____

_____

LOCATION_____DATE_____

DIRECTIONS_____

_____

_____

WATER LEVEL_____

ROD_____

TECHNIQUE:_____DRY_____NYMPH_____STREAMER

SPECIES_____( )   SPECIES_____( )

SPECIES_____( )   SPECIES_____( )

BEST FLY_____

ADDITIONAL NOTES_____

_____

LOCATION_____DATE_____

DIRECTIONS_____

_____

_____

WATER LEVEL_____

ROD_____

TECHNIQUE:_____DRY_____NYMPH_____STREAMER

SPECIES_____( )   SPECIES_____( )

SPECIES_____( )   SPECIES_____( )

BEST FLY_____

ADDITIONAL NOTES_____

_____

LOCATION_____DATE_____

DIRECTIONS_____

_____

_____

WATER LEVEL_____

ROD_____

TECHNIQUE:_____DRY_____NYMPH_____STREAMER

SPECIES_____( )   SPECIES_____( )

SPECIES_____( )   SPECIES_____( )

BEST FLY_____

ADDITIONAL NOTES_____

_____

LOCATION_____DATE_____

DIRECTIONS_____

_____

_____

WATER LEVEL_____

ROD_____

TECHNIQUE:_____DRY_____NYMPH_____STREAMER

SPECIES_____( )   SPECIES_____( )

SPECIES_____( )   SPECIES_____( )

BEST FLY_____

ADDITIONAL NOTES_____

_____

LOCATION_____DATE_____

DIRECTIONS_____

_____

_____

WATER LEVEL_____

ROD_____

TECHNIQUE:_____DRY_____NYMPH_____STREAMER

SPECIES_____( )   SPECIES_____( )

SPECIES_____( )   SPECIES_____( )

BEST FLY_____

ADDITIONAL NOTES_____

_____

LOCATION_____DATE_____

DIRECTIONS_____

_____

_____

WATER LEVEL_____

ROD_____

TECHNIQUE:_____DRY_____NYMPH_____STREAMER

SPECIES_____( )   SPECIES_____( )

SPECIES_____( )   SPECIES_____( )

BEST FLY_____

ADDITIONAL NOTES_____

_____

LOCATION_____DATE_____

DIRECTIONS_____

_____

_____

WATER LEVEL_____

ROD_____

TECHNIQUE:_____DRY_____NYMPH_____STREAMER

SPECIES_____( )   SPECIES_____( )

SPECIES_____( )   SPECIES_____( )

BEST FLY_____

ADDITIONAL NOTES_____

_____

LOCATION_____DATE_____

DIRECTIONS_____

_____

_____

WATER LEVEL_____

ROD_____

TECHNIQUE:_____DRY_____NYMPH_____STREAMER

SPECIES_____( )   SPECIES_____( )

SPECIES_____( )   SPECIES_____( )

BEST FLY_____

ADDITIONAL NOTES_____

_____

LOCATION_____DATE_____
DIRECTIONS_____
_____
_____
WATER LEVEL_____
ROD_____
TECHNIQUE:_____DRY_____NYMPH_____STREAMER
SPECIES_____( )   SPECIES_____( )
SPECIES_____( )   SPECIES_____( )
BEST FLY_____
ADDITIONAL NOTES_____
_____

LOCATION_____DATE_____
DIRECTIONS_____
_____
_____
WATER LEVEL_____
ROD_____
TECHNIQUE:_____DRY_____NYMPH_____STREAMER
SPECIES_____( )   SPECIES_____( )
SPECIES_____( )   SPECIES_____( )
BEST FLY_____
ADDITIONAL NOTES_____
_____

LOCATION_____DATE_____

DIRECTIONS_____

_____

_____

WATER LEVEL_____

ROD_____

TECHNIQUE:_____DRY_____NYMPH_____STREAMER

SPECIES_____( )   SPECIES_____( )

SPECIES_____( )   SPECIES_____( )

BEST FLY_____

ADDITIONAL NOTES_____

_____

LOCATION_____DATE_____

DIRECTIONS_____

_____

_____

WATER LEVEL_____

ROD_____

TECHNIQUE:_____DRY_____NYMPH_____STREAMER

SPECIES_____( )   SPECIES_____( )

SPECIES_____( )   SPECIES_____( )

BEST FLY_____

ADDITIONAL NOTES_____

_____

LOCATION_____DATE_____

DIRECTIONS_____

_____

_____

WATER LEVEL_____

ROD_____

TECHNIQUE:_____DRY_____NYMPH_____STREAMER

SPECIES_____( )   SPECIES_____( )

SPECIES_____( )   SPECIES_____( )

BEST FLY_____

ADDITIONAL NOTES_____

_____

LOCATION_____DATE_____

DIRECTIONS_____

_____

_____

WATER LEVEL_____

ROD_____

TECHNIQUE:_____DRY_____NYMPH_____STREAMER

SPECIES_____( )   SPECIES_____( )

SPECIES_____( )   SPECIES_____( )

BEST FLY_____

ADDITIONAL NOTES_____

_____

LOCATION_____DATE_____

DIRECTIONS_____

_____

_____

WATER LEVEL_____

ROD_____

TECHNIQUE:_____DRY_____NYMPH_____STREAMER

SPECIES_____( )   SPECIES_____( )

SPECIES_____( )   SPECIES_____( )

BEST FLY_____

ADDITIONAL NOTES_____

_____

LOCATION_____DATE_____

DIRECTIONS_____

_____

_____

WATER LEVEL_____

ROD_____

TECHNIQUE:_____DRY_____NYMPH_____STREAMER

SPECIES_____( )   SPECIES_____( )

SPECIES_____( )   SPECIES_____( )

BEST FLY_____

ADDITIONAL NOTES_____

_____

LOCATION_____DATE_____
DIRECTIONS_____
_____
_____
WATER LEVEL_____
ROD_____
TECHNIQUE:_____DRY_____NYMPH_____STREAMER
SPECIES_____( )   SPECIES_____( )
SPECIES_____( )   SPECIES_____( )
BEST FLY_____
ADDITIONAL NOTES_____
_____

LOCATION_____DATE_____
DIRECTIONS_____
_____
_____
WATER LEVEL_____
ROD_____
TECHNIQUE:_____DRY_____NYMPH_____STREAMER
SPECIES_____( )   SPECIES_____( )
SPECIES_____( )   SPECIES_____( )
BEST FLY_____
ADDITIONAL NOTES_____
_____

LOCATION_____DATE_____

DIRECTIONS_____

_____

_____

WATER LEVEL_____

ROD_____

TECHNIQUE:_____DRY_____NYMPH_____STREAMER

SPECIES_____( )   SPECIES_____( )

SPECIES_____( )   SPECIES_____( )

BEST FLY_____

ADDITIONAL NOTES_____

_____

LOCATION_____DATE_____

DIRECTIONS_____

_____

_____

WATER LEVEL_____

ROD_____

TECHNIQUE:_____DRY_____NYMPH_____STREAMER

SPECIES_____( )   SPECIES_____( )

SPECIES_____( )   SPECIES_____( )

BEST FLY_____

ADDITIONAL NOTES_____

_____

LOCATION_____DATE_____

DIRECTIONS_____

_____

_____

WATER LEVEL_____

ROD_____

TECHNIQUE:_____DRY_____NYMPH_____STREAMER

SPECIES_____( )   SPECIES_____( )

SPECIES_____( )   SPECIES_____( )

BEST FLY_____

ADDITIONAL NOTES_____

_____

LOCATION_____DATE_____

DIRECTIONS_____

_____

_____

WATER LEVEL_____

ROD_____

TECHNIQUE:_____DRY_____NYMPH_____STREAMER

SPECIES_____( )   SPECIES_____( )

SPECIES_____( )   SPECIES_____( )

BEST FLY_____

ADDITIONAL NOTES_____

_____

LOCATION_____DATE_____
DIRECTIONS_____
_____
_____
WATER LEVEL_____
ROD_____
TECHNIQUE:_____DRY_____NYMPH_____STREAMER
SPECIES_____( )   SPECIES_____( )
SPECIES_____( )   SPECIES_____( )
BEST FLY_____
ADDITIONAL NOTES_____
_____

LOCATION_____DATE_____
DIRECTIONS_____
_____
_____
WATER LEVEL_____
ROD_____
TECHNIQUE:_____DRY_____NYMPH_____STREAMER
SPECIES_____( )   SPECIES_____( )
SPECIES_____( )   SPECIES_____( )
BEST FLY_____
ADDITIONAL NOTES_____
_____

LOCATION_____DATE_____

DIRECTIONS_____

_____

_____

WATER LEVEL_____

ROD_____

TECHNIQUE:_____DRY_____NYMPH_____STREAMER

SPECIES_____( )   SPECIES_____( )

SPECIES_____( )   SPECIES_____( )

BEST FLY_____

ADDITIONAL NOTES_____

_____

LOCATION_____DATE_____

DIRECTIONS_____

_____

_____

WATER LEVEL_____

ROD_____

TECHNIQUE:_____DRY_____NYMPH_____STREAMER

SPECIES_____( )   SPECIES_____( )

SPECIES_____( )   SPECIES_____( )

BEST FLY_____

ADDITIONAL NOTES_____

_____

LOCATION_____DATE_____

DIRECTIONS_____

_____

_____

WATER LEVEL_____

ROD_____

TECHNIQUE:_____DRY_____NYMPH_____STREAMER

SPECIES_____( )   SPECIES_____( )

SPECIES_____( )   SPECIES_____( )

BEST FLY_____

ADDITIONAL NOTES_____

_____

LOCATION_____DATE_____

DIRECTIONS_____

_____

_____

WATER LEVEL_____

ROD_____

TECHNIQUE:_____DRY_____NYMPH_____STREAMER

SPECIES_____( )   SPECIES_____( )

SPECIES_____( )   SPECIES_____( )

BEST FLY_____

ADDITIONAL NOTES_____

_____

LOCATION_____DATE_____

DIRECTIONS_____

_____

_____

WATER LEVEL_____

ROD_____

TECHNIQUE:_____DRY_____NYMPH_____STREAMER

SPECIES_____( )   SPECIES_____( )

SPECIES_____( )   SPECIES_____( )

BEST FLY_____

ADDITIONAL NOTES_____

_____

LOCATION_____DATE_____

DIRECTIONS_____

_____

_____

WATER LEVEL_____

ROD_____

TECHNIQUE:_____DRY_____NYMPH_____STREAMER

SPECIES_____( )   SPECIES_____( )

SPECIES_____( )   SPECIES_____( )

BEST FLY_____

ADDITIONAL NOTES_____

_____

LOCATION_____DATE_____

DIRECTIONS_____

_____

_____

WATER LEVEL_____

ROD_____

TECHNIQUE:_____DRY_____NYMPH_____STREAMER

SPECIES_____( )   SPECIES_____( )

SPECIES_____( )   SPECIES_____( )

BEST FLY_____

ADDITIONAL NOTES_____

_____

LOCATION_____DATE_____

DIRECTIONS_____

_____

_____

WATER LEVEL_____

ROD_____

TECHNIQUE:_____DRY_____NYMPH_____STREAMER

SPECIES_____( )   SPECIES_____( )

SPECIES_____( )   SPECIES_____( )

BEST FLY_____

ADDITIONAL NOTES_____

_____

LOCATION_____DATE_____

DIRECTIONS_____

_____

_____

WATER LEVEL_____

ROD_____

TECHNIQUE:_____DRY_____NYMPH_____STREAMER

SPECIES_____( )   SPECIES_____( )

SPECIES_____( )   SPECIES_____( )

BEST FLY_____

ADDITIONAL NOTES_____

_____

LOCATION_____DATE_____

DIRECTIONS_____

_____

_____

WATER LEVEL_____

ROD_____

TECHNIQUE:_____DRY_____NYMPH_____STREAMER

SPECIES_____( )   SPECIES_____( )

SPECIES_____( )   SPECIES_____( )

BEST FLY_____

ADDITIONAL NOTES_____

_____

LOCATION_____DATE_____

DIRECTIONS_____

_____

_____

WATER LEVEL_____

ROD_____

TECHNIQUE:_____DRY_____NYMPH_____STREAMER

SPECIES_____( )   SPECIES_____( )

SPECIES_____( )   SPECIES_____( )

BEST FLY_____

ADDITIONAL NOTES_____

_____

LOCATION_____DATE_____

DIRECTIONS_____

_____

_____

WATER LEVEL_____

ROD_____

TECHNIQUE:_____DRY_____NYMPH_____STREAMER

SPECIES_____( )   SPECIES_____( )

SPECIES_____( )   SPECIES_____( )

BEST FLY_____

ADDITIONAL NOTES_____

_____

LOCATION_____DATE_____

DIRECTIONS_____

_____

_____

WATER LEVEL_____

ROD_____

TECHNIQUE:_____DRY_____NYMPH_____STREAMER

SPECIES_____( )   SPECIES_____( )

SPECIES_____( )   SPECIES_____( )

BEST FLY_____

ADDITIONAL NOTES_____

_____

LOCATION_____DATE_____

DIRECTIONS_____

_____

_____

WATER LEVEL_____

ROD_____

TECHNIQUE:_____DRY_____NYMPH_____STREAMER

SPECIES_____( )   SPECIES_____( )

SPECIES_____( )   SPECIES_____( )

BEST FLY_____

ADDITIONAL NOTES_____

_____

LOCATION_____DATE_____

DIRECTIONS_____

_____

_____

WATER LEVEL_____

ROD_____

TECHNIQUE:_____DRY_____NYMPH_____STREAMER

SPECIES_____( )   SPECIES_____( )

SPECIES_____( )   SPECIES_____( )

BEST FLY_____

ADDITIONAL NOTES_____

_____

LOCATION_____DATE_____

DIRECTIONS_____

_____

_____

WATER LEVEL_____

ROD_____

TECHNIQUE:_____DRY_____NYMPH_____STREAMER

SPECIES_____( )   SPECIES_____( )

SPECIES_____( )   SPECIES_____( )

BEST FLY_____

ADDITIONAL NOTES_____

_____

LOCATION_____DATE_____

DIRECTIONS_____

_____

_____

WATER LEVEL_____

ROD_____

TECHNIQUE:_____DRY_____NYMPH_____STREAMER

SPECIES_____( )   SPECIES_____( )

SPECIES_____( )   SPECIES_____( )

BEST FLY_____

ADDITIONAL NOTES_____

_____

LOCATION_____DATE_____

DIRECTIONS_____

_____

_____

WATER LEVEL_____

ROD_____

TECHNIQUE:_____DRY_____NYMPH_____STREAMER

SPECIES_____( )   SPECIES_____( )

SPECIES_____( )   SPECIES_____( )

BEST FLY_____

ADDITIONAL NOTES_____

_____

LOCATION_____DATE_____
DIRECTIONS_____
_____
_____
WATER LEVEL_____
ROD_____
TECHNIQUE:_____DRY_____NYMPH_____STREAMER
SPECIES_____( ) SPECIES_____( )
SPECIES_____( ) SPECIES_____( )
BEST FLY_____
ADDITIONAL NOTES_____
_____

LOCATION_____DATE_____
DIRECTIONS_____
_____
_____
WATER LEVEL_____
ROD_____
TECHNIQUE:_____DRY_____NYMPH_____STREAMER
SPECIES_____( ) SPECIES_____( )
SPECIES_____( ) SPECIES_____( )
BEST FLY_____
ADDITIONAL NOTES_____
_____

LOCATION_____DATE_____

DIRECTIONS_____

_____

_____

WATER LEVEL_____

ROD_____

TECHNIQUE:_____DRY_____NYMPH_____STREAMER

SPECIES_____( )   SPECIES_____( )

SPECIES_____( )   SPECIES_____( )

BEST FLY_____

ADDITIONAL NOTES_____

_____

LOCATION_____DATE_____

DIRECTIONS_____

_____

_____

WATER LEVEL_____

ROD_____

TECHNIQUE:_____DRY_____NYMPH_____STREAMER

SPECIES_____( )   SPECIES_____( )

SPECIES_____( )   SPECIES_____( )

BEST FLY_____

ADDITIONAL NOTES_____

_____

LOCATION_____DATE_____

DIRECTIONS_____

_____

_____

WATER LEVEL_____

ROD_____

TECHNIQUE:_____DRY_____NYMPH_____STREAMER

SPECIES_____( )   SPECIES_____( )

SPECIES_____( )   SPECIES_____( )

BEST FLY_____

ADDITIONAL NOTES_____

_____

LOCATION_____DATE_____

DIRECTIONS_____

_____

_____

WATER LEVEL_____

ROD_____

TECHNIQUE:_____DRY_____NYMPH_____STREAMER

SPECIES_____( )   SPECIES_____( )

SPECIES_____( )   SPECIES_____( )

BEST FLY_____

ADDITIONAL NOTES_____

_____

LOCATION_____DATE_____

DIRECTIONS_____

_____

_____

WATER LEVEL_____

ROD_____

TECHNIQUE:_____DRY_____NYMPH_____STREAMER

SPECIES_____( )   SPECIES_____( )

SPECIES_____( )   SPECIES_____( )

BEST FLY_____

ADDITIONAL NOTES_____

_____

LOCATION_____DATE_____

DIRECTIONS_____

_____

_____

WATER LEVEL_____

ROD_____

TECHNIQUE:_____DRY_____NYMPH_____STREAMER

SPECIES_____( )   SPECIES_____( )

SPECIES_____( )   SPECIES_____( )

BEST FLY_____

ADDITIONAL NOTES_____

_____

LOCATION_____DATE_____

DIRECTIONS_____

_____

_____

WATER LEVEL_____

ROD_____

TECHNIQUE:_____DRY_____NYMPH_____STREAMER

SPECIES_____( )   SPECIES_____( )

SPECIES_____( )   SPECIES_____( )

BEST FLY_____

ADDITIONAL NOTES_____

_____

LOCATION_____DATE_____

DIRECTIONS_____

_____

_____

WATER LEVEL_____

ROD_____

TECHNIQUE:_____DRY_____NYMPH_____STREAMER

SPECIES_____( )   SPECIES_____( )

SPECIES_____( )   SPECIES_____( )

BEST FLY_____

ADDITIONAL NOTES_____

_____

LOCATION_____DATE_____
DIRECTIONS_____
_____
_____
WATER LEVEL_____
ROD_____
TECHNIQUE:_____DRY_____NYMPH_____STREAMER
SPECIES_____( )   SPECIES_____( )

SPECIES_____( )   SPECIES_____( )

BEST FLY_____

ADDITIONAL NOTES_____

_____

LOCATION_____DATE_____
DIRECTIONS_____
_____
_____
WATER LEVEL_____
ROD_____
TECHNIQUE:_____DRY_____NYMPH_____STREAMER
SPECIES_____( )   SPECIES_____( )

SPECIES_____( )   SPECIES_____( )

BEST FLY_____

ADDITIONAL NOTES_____

_____

LOCATION_____DATE_____

DIRECTIONS_____

_____

_____

WATER LEVEL_____

ROD_____

TECHNIQUE:_____DRY_____NYMPH_____STREAMER

SPECIES_____( ) SPECIES_____( )

SPECIES_____( ) SPECIES_____( )

BEST FLY_____

ADDITIONAL NOTES_____

_____

LOCATION_____DATE_____

DIRECTIONS_____

_____

_____

WATER LEVEL_____

ROD_____

TECHNIQUE:_____DRY_____NYMPH_____STREAMER

SPECIES_____( ) SPECIES_____( )

SPECIES_____( ) SPECIES_____( )

BEST FLY_____

ADDITIONAL NOTES_____

_____

LOCATION_____DATE_____

DIRECTIONS_____

_____

_____

WATER LEVEL_____

ROD_____

TECHNIQUE:_____DRY_____NYMPH_____STREAMER

SPECIES_____( )   SPECIES_____( )

SPECIES_____( ). SPECIES_____( )

BEST FLY_____

ADDITIONAL NOTES_____

_____

LOCATION_____DATE_____

DIRECTIONS_____

_____

_____

WATER LEVEL_____

ROD_____

TECHNIQUE:_____DRY_____NYMPH_____STREAMER

SPECIES_____( )   SPECIES_____( )

SPECIES_____( )   SPECIES_____( )

BEST FLY_____

ADDITIONAL NOTES_____

_____

LOCATION_____DATE_____

DIRECTIONS_____

_____

_____

WATER LEVEL_____

ROD_____

TECHNIQUE:_____DRY_____NYMPH_____STREAMER

SPECIES_____( )   SPECIES_____( )

SPECIES_____( )   SPECIES_____( )

BEST FLY_____

ADDITIONAL NOTES_____

_____

LOCATION_____DATE_____

DIRECTIONS_____

_____

_____

WATER LEVEL_____

ROD_____

TECHNIQUE:_____DRY_____NYMPH_____STREAMER

SPECIES_____( )   SPECIES_____( )

SPECIES_____( )   SPECIES_____( )

BEST FLY_____

ADDITIONAL NOTES_____

_____

LOCATION_____DATE_____

DIRECTIONS_____

_____

_____

WATER LEVEL_____

ROD_____

TECHNIQUE:_____DRY_____NYMPH_____STREAMER

SPECIES_____( )   SPECIES_____( )

SPECIES_____( )   SPECIES_____( )

BEST FLY_____

ADDITIONAL NOTES_____

_____

LOCATION_____DATE_____

DIRECTIONS_____

_____

_____

WATER LEVEL_____

ROD_____

TECHNIQUE:_____DRY_____NYMPH_____STREAMER

SPECIES_____( )   SPECIES_____( )

SPECIES_____( )   SPECIES_____( )

BEST FLY_____

ADDITIONAL NOTES_____

_____

LOCATION_____DATE_____

DIRECTIONS_____

_____

_____

WATER LEVEL_____

ROD_____

TECHNIQUE:_____DRY_____NYMPH_____STREAMER

SPECIES_____( )   SPECIES_____( )

SPECIES_____( )   SPECIES_____( )

BEST FLY_____

ADDITIONAL NOTES_____

_____

LOCATION_____DATE_____

DIRECTIONS_____

_____

_____

WATER LEVEL_____

ROD_____

TECHNIQUE:_____DRY_____NYMPH_____STREAMER

SPECIES_____( )   SPECIES_____( )

SPECIES_____( )   SPECIES_____( )

BEST FLY_____

ADDITIONAL NOTES_____

_____

LOCATION_____DATE_____

DIRECTIONS_____

_____

_____

WATER LEVEL_____

ROD_____

TECHNIQUE:_____DRY_____NYMPH_____STREAMER

SPECIES_____( ) SPECIES_____( )

SPECIES_____( ) SPECIES_____( )

BEST FLY_____

ADDITIONAL NOTES_____

_____

LOCATION_____DATE_____

DIRECTIONS_____

_____

_____

WATER LEVEL_____

ROD_____

TECHNIQUE:_____DRY_____NYMPH_____STREAMER

SPECIES_____( ) SPECIES_____( )

SPECIES_____( ) SPECIES_____( )

BEST FLY_____

ADDITIONAL NOTES_____

_____

LOCATION_____DATE_____

DIRECTIONS_____

_____

_____

WATER LEVEL_____

ROD_____

TECHNIQUE:_____DRY_____NYMPH_____STREAMER

SPECIES_____( )   SPECIES_____( )

SPECIES_____( )   SPECIES_____( )

BEST FLY_____

ADDITIONAL NOTES_____

_____

LOCATION_____DATE_____

DIRECTIONS_____

_____

_____

WATER LEVEL_____

ROD_____

TECHNIQUE:_____DRY_____NYMPH_____STREAMER

SPECIES_____( )   SPECIES_____( )

SPECIES_____( )   SPECIES_____( )

BEST FLY_____

ADDITIONAL NOTES_____

_____

LOCATION_____DATE_____
DIRECTIONS_____
_____
_____
WATER LEVEL_____
ROD_____
TECHNIQUE:_____DRY_____NYMPH_____STREAMER
SPECIES_____( )   SPECIES_____( )

SPECIES_____( )   SPECIES_____( )

BEST FLY_____
ADDITIONAL NOTES_____
_____

LOCATION_____DATE_____
DIRECTIONS_____
_____
_____
WATER LEVEL_____
ROD_____
TECHNIQUE:_____DRY_____NYMPH_____STREAMER
SPECIES_____( )   SPECIES_____( )

SPECIES_____( )   SPECIES_____( )

BEST FLY_____
ADDITIONAL NOTES_____
_____

LOCATION_____DATE_____

DIRECTIONS_____

_____

_____

WATER LEVEL_____

ROD_____

TECHNIQUE:_____DRY_____NYMPH_____STREAMER

SPECIES_____( )   SPECIES_____( )

SPECIES_____( )   SPECIES_____( )

BEST FLY_____

ADDITIONAL NOTES_____

_____

LOCATION_____DATE_____

DIRECTIONS_____

_____

_____

WATER LEVEL_____

ROD_____

TECHNIQUE:_____DRY_____NYMPH_____STREAMER

SPECIES_____( )   SPECIES_____( )

SPECIES_____( )   SPECIES_____( )

BEST FLY_____

ADDITIONAL NOTES_____

_____

LOCATION_____DATE_____

DIRECTIONS_____

_____

_____

WATER LEVEL_____

ROD_____

TECHNIQUE:_____DRY_____NYMPH_____STREAMER

SPECIES_____( )   SPECIES_____( )

SPECIES_____( )   SPECIES_____( )

BEST FLY_____

ADDITIONAL NOTES_____

_____

LOCATION_____DATE_____

DIRECTIONS_____

_____

_____

WATER LEVEL_____

ROD_____

TECHNIQUE:_____DRY_____NYMPH_____STREAMER

SPECIES_____( )   SPECIES_____( )

SPECIES_____( )   SPECIES_____( )

BEST FLY_____

ADDITIONAL NOTES_____

_____

LOCATION_____DATE_____

DIRECTIONS_____

_____

_____

WATER LEVEL_____

ROD_____

TECHNIQUE:_____DRY_____NYMPH_____STREAMER

SPECIES_____( )   SPECIES_____( )

SPECIES_____( )   SPECIES_____( )

BEST FLY_____

ADDITIONAL NOTES_____

_____

LOCATION_____DATE_____

DIRECTIONS_____

_____

_____

WATER LEVEL_____

ROD_____

TECHNIQUE:_____DRY_____NYMPH_____STREAMER

SPECIES_____( )   SPECIES_____( )

SPECIES_____( )   SPECIES_____( )

BEST FLY_____

ADDITIONAL NOTES_____

_____

LOCATION_____DATE_____

DIRECTIONS_____

_____

_____

WATER LEVEL_____

ROD_____

TECHNIQUE:_____DRY_____NYMPH_____STREAMER

SPECIES_____( )   SPECIES_____( )

SPECIES_____( )   SPECIES_____( )

BEST FLY_____

ADDITIONAL NOTES_____

_____

LOCATION_____DATE_____

DIRECTIONS_____

_____

_____

WATER LEVEL_____

ROD_____

TECHNIQUE:_____DRY_____NYMPH_____STREAMER

SPECIES_____( )   SPECIES_____( )

SPECIES_____( )   SPECIES_____( )

BEST FLY_____

ADDITIONAL NOTES_____

_____

LOCATION_____DATE_____

DIRECTIONS_____

_____

_____

WATER LEVEL_____

ROD_____

TECHNIQUE:_____DRY_____NYMPH_____STREAMER

SPECIES_____( )   SPECIES_____( )

SPECIES_____( )   SPECIES_____( )

BEST FLY_____

ADDITIONAL NOTES_____

_____

LOCATION_____DATE_____

DIRECTIONS_____

_____

_____

WATER LEVEL_____

ROD_____

TECHNIQUE:_____DRY_____NYMPH_____STREAMER

SPECIES_____( )   SPECIES_____( )

SPECIES_____( )   SPECIES_____( )

BEST FLY_____

ADDITIONAL NOTES_____

_____

LOCATION_____DATE_____

DIRECTIONS_____

_____

_____

WATER LEVEL_____

ROD_____

TECHNIQUE:_____DRY_____NYMPH_____STREAMER

SPECIES_____( )   SPECIES_____( )

SPECIES_____( )   SPECIES_____( )

BEST FLY_____

ADDITIONAL NOTES_____

_____

LOCATION_____DATE_____

DIRECTIONS_____

_____

_____

WATER LEVEL_____

ROD_____

TECHNIQUE:_____DRY_____NYMPH_____STREAMER

SPECIES_____( )   SPECIES_____( )

SPECIES_____( )   SPECIES_____( )

BEST FLY_____

ADDITIONAL NOTES_____

_____

LOCATION_____DATE_____

DIRECTIONS_____

_____

_____

WATER LEVEL_____

ROD_____

TECHNIQUE:_____DRY_____NYMPH_____STREAMER

SPECIES_____( )   SPECIES_____( )

SPECIES_____( )   SPECIES_____( )

BEST FLY_____

ADDITIONAL NOTES_____

_____

LOCATION_____DATE_____

DIRECTIONS_____

_____

_____

WATER LEVEL_____

ROD_____

TECHNIQUE:_____DRY_____NYMPH_____STREAMER

SPECIES_____( )   SPECIES_____( )

SPECIES_____( )   SPECIES_____( )

BEST FLY_____

ADDITIONAL NOTES_____

_____

LOCATION_____DATE_____

DIRECTIONS_____

_____

_____

WATER LEVEL_____

ROD_____

TECHNIQUE:_____DRY_____NYMPH_____STREAMER

SPECIES_____( )   SPECIES_____( )

SPECIES_____( )   SPECIES_____( )

BEST FLY_____

ADDITIONAL NOTES_____

_____

LOCATION_____DATE_____

DIRECTIONS_____

_____

_____

WATER LEVEL_____

ROD_____

TECHNIQUE:_____DRY_____NYMPH_____STREAMER

SPECIES_____( )   SPECIES_____( )

SPECIES_____( )   SPECIES_____( )

BEST FLY_____

ADDITIONAL NOTES_____

_____

LOCATION_____DATE_____

DIRECTIONS_____

_____

_____

WATER LEVEL_____

ROD_____

TECHNIQUE:_____DRY_____NYMPH_____STREAMER

SPECIES_____( )   SPECIES_____( )

SPECIES_____( )   SPECIES_____( )

BEST FLY_____

ADDITIONAL NOTES_____

_____

LOCATION_____DATE_____

DIRECTIONS_____

_____

_____

WATER LEVEL_____

ROD_____

TECHNIQUE:_____DRY_____NYMPH_____STREAMER

SPECIES_____( )   SPECIES_____( )

SPECIES_____( )   SPECIES_____( )

BEST FLY_____

ADDITIONAL NOTES_____

_____

LOCATION_____DATE_____

DIRECTIONS_____

_____

_____

WATER LEVEL_____

ROD_____

TECHNIQUE:_____DRY_____NYMPH_____STREAMER

SPECIES_____( )   SPECIES_____( )

SPECIES_____( )   SPECIES_____( )

BEST FLY_____

ADDITIONAL NOTES_____

_____

LOCATION_____DATE_____

DIRECTIONS_____

_____

_____

WATER LEVEL_____

ROD_____

TECHNIQUE:_____DRY_____NYMPH_____STREAMER

SPECIES_____( )   SPECIES_____( )

SPECIES_____( )   SPECIES_____( )

BEST FLY_____

ADDITIONAL NOTES_____

_____

LOCATION_____DATE_____

DIRECTIONS_____

_____

_____

WATER LEVEL_____

ROD_____

TECHNIQUE:_____DRY_____NYMPH_____STREAMER

SPECIES_____( )   SPECIES_____( )

SPECIES_____( )   SPECIES_____( )

BEST FLY_____

ADDITIONAL NOTES_____

_____

LOCATION_____DATE_____

DIRECTIONS_____

_____

_____

WATER LEVEL_____

ROD_____

TECHNIQUE:_____DRY_____NYMPH_____STREAMER

SPECIES_____( )   SPECIES_____( )

SPECIES_____( )   SPECIES_____( )

BEST FLY_____

ADDITIONAL NOTES_____

_____

LOCATION_____DATE_____

DIRECTIONS_____

_____

_____

WATER LEVEL_____

ROD_____

TECHNIQUE:_____DRY_____NYMPH_____STREAMER

SPECIES_____( )   SPECIES_____( )

SPECIES_____( )   SPECIES_____( )

BEST FLY_____

ADDITIONAL NOTES_____

_____

LOCATION_____DATE_____

DIRECTIONS_____

_____

_____

WATER LEVEL_____

ROD_____

TECHNIQUE:_____DRY_____NYMPH_____STREAMER

SPECIES_____( )   SPECIES_____( )

SPECIES_____( )   SPECIES_____( )

BEST FLY_____

ADDITIONAL NOTES_____

_____

LOCATION_____DATE_____

DIRECTIONS_____

_____

_____

WATER LEVEL_____

ROD_____

TECHNIQUE:_____DRY_____NYMPH_____STREAMER

SPECIES_____( )   SPECIES_____( )

SPECIES_____( )   SPECIES_____( )

BEST FLY_____

ADDITIONAL NOTES_____

_____

LOCATION_____DATE_____

DIRECTIONS_____

_____

_____

WATER LEVEL_____

ROD_____

TECHNIQUE:_____DRY_____NYMPH_____STREAMER

SPECIES_____( )   SPECIES_____( )

SPECIES_____( )   SPECIES_____( )

BEST FLY_____

ADDITIONAL NOTES_____

_____

LOCATION_____DATE_____

DIRECTIONS_____

_____

_____

WATER LEVEL_____

ROD_____

TECHNIQUE:_____DRY_____NYMPH_____STREAMER

SPECIES_____( )   SPECIES_____( )

SPECIES_____( )   SPECIES_____( )

BEST FLY_____

ADDITIONAL NOTES_____

_____

LOCATION_____DATE_____

DIRECTIONS_____

_____

_____

WATER LEVEL_____

ROD_____

TECHNIQUE:_____DRY_____NYMPH_____STREAMER

SPECIES_____( )   SPECIES_____( )

SPECIES_____( )   SPECIES_____( )

BEST FLY_____

ADDITIONAL NOTES_____

_____

LOCATION_____DATE_____

DIRECTIONS_____

_____

_____

WATER LEVEL_____

ROD_____

TECHNIQUE:_____DRY_____NYMPH_____STREAMER

SPECIES_____( )   SPECIES_____( )

SPECIES_____( )   SPECIES_____( )

BEST FLY_____

ADDITIONAL NOTES_____

_____

LOCATION_____DATE_____

DIRECTIONS_____

_____

_____

WATER LEVEL_____

ROD_____

TECHNIQUE:_____DRY_____NYMPH_____STREAMER

SPECIES_____( )   SPECIES_____( )

SPECIES_____( )   SPECIES_____( )

BEST FLY_____

ADDITIONAL NOTES_____

_____

LOCATION_____DATE_____

DIRECTIONS_____

_____

_____

WATER LEVEL_____

ROD_____

TECHNIQUE:_____DRY_____NYMPH_____STREAMER

SPECIES_____( )   SPECIES_____( )

SPECIES_____( )   SPECIES_____( )

BEST FLY_____

ADDITIONAL NOTES_____

_____

LOCATION_____DATE_____

DIRECTIONS_____

_____

_____

WATER LEVEL_____

ROD_____

TECHNIQUE:_____DRY_____NYMPH_____STREAMER

SPECIES_____( )   SPECIES_____( )

SPECIES_____( )   SPECIES_____( )

BEST FLY_____

ADDITIONAL NOTES_____

_____

LOCATION_____DATE_____

DIRECTIONS_____

_____

_____

WATER LEVEL_____

ROD_____

TECHNIQUE:_____DRY_____NYMPH_____STREAMER

SPECIES_____( )   SPECIES_____( )

SPECIES_____( )   SPECIES_____( )

BEST FLY_____

ADDITIONAL NOTES_____

_____

LOCATION_____DATE_____

DIRECTIONS_____

_____

_____

WATER LEVEL_____

ROD_____

TECHNIQUE:_____DRY_____NYMPH_____STREAMER

SPECIES_____( )   SPECIES_____( )

SPECIES_____( )   SPECIES_____( )

BEST FLY_____

ADDITIONAL NOTES_____

_____

LOCATION_____DATE_____

DIRECTIONS_____

_____

_____

WATER LEVEL_____

ROD_____

TECHNIQUE:_____DRY_____NYMPH_____STREAMER

SPECIES_____( )   SPECIES_____( )

SPECIES_____( )   SPECIES_____( )

BEST FLY_____

ADDITIONAL NOTES_____

_____

LOCATION_____DATE_____

DIRECTIONS_____

_____

_____

WATER LEVEL_____

ROD_____

TECHNIQUE:_____DRY_____NYMPH_____STREAMER

SPECIES_____( )   SPECIES_____( )

SPECIES_____( )   SPECIES_____( )

BEST FLY_____

ADDITIONAL NOTES_____

_____

LOCATION_____DATE_____

DIRECTIONS_____

_____

_____

WATER LEVEL_____

ROD_____

TECHNIQUE:_____DRY_____NYMPH_____STREAMER

SPECIES_____( )   SPECIES_____( )

SPECIES_____( )   SPECIES_____( )

BEST FLY_____

ADDITIONAL NOTES_____

_____

LOCATION_____DATE_____

DIRECTIONS_____

_____

_____

WATER LEVEL_____

ROD_____

TECHNIQUE:_____DRY_____NYMPH_____STREAMER

SPECIES_____( )   SPECIES_____( )

SPECIES_____( )   SPECIES_____( )

BEST FLY_____

ADDITIONAL NOTES_____

_____

LOCATION_____DATE_____

DIRECTIONS_____

_____

_____

WATER LEVEL_____

ROD_____

TECHNIQUE:_____DRY_____NYMPH_____STREAMER

SPECIES_____( )   SPECIES_____( )

SPECIES_____( )   SPECIES_____( )

BEST FLY_____

ADDITIONAL NOTES_____

_____

LOCATION_____DATE_____

DIRECTIONS_____

_____

_____

WATER LEVEL_____

ROD_____

TECHNIQUE:_____DRY_____NYMPH_____STREAMER

SPECIES_____( )   SPECIES_____( )

SPECIES_____( )   SPECIES_____( )

BEST FLY_____

ADDITIONAL NOTES_____

_____

LOCATION_____DATE_____
DIRECTIONS_____
_____
_____
WATER LEVEL_____
ROD_____
TECHNIQUE:_____DRY_____NYMPH_____STREAMER
SPECIES_____( )   SPECIES_____( )
SPECIES_____( )   SPECIES_____( )
BEST FLY_____
ADDITIONAL NOTES_____
_____

LOCATION_____DATE_____
DIRECTIONS_____
_____
_____
WATER LEVEL_____
ROD_____
TECHNIQUE:_____DRY_____NYMPH_____STREAMER
SPECIES_____( )   SPECIES_____( )
SPECIES_____( )   SPECIES_____( )
BEST FLY_____
ADDITIONAL NOTES_____
_____

LOCATION_____DATE_____
DIRECTIONS_____
_____
_____
WATER LEVEL_____
ROD_____
TECHNIQUE:_____DRY_____NYMPH_____STREAMER
SPECIES_____( )   SPECIES_____( )
SPECIES_____( )   SPECIES_____( )
BEST FLY_____
ADDITIONAL NOTES_____
_____

LOCATION_____DATE_____
DIRECTIONS_____
_____
_____
WATER LEVEL_____
ROD_____
TECHNIQUE:_____DRY_____NYMPH_____STREAMER
SPECIES_____( )   SPECIES_____( )
SPECIES_____( )   SPECIES_____( )
BEST FLY_____
ADDITIONAL NOTES_____
_____

LOCATION_____DATE_____

DIRECTIONS_____

_____

_____

WATER LEVEL_____

ROD_____

TECHNIQUE:_____DRY_____NYMPH_____STREAMER

SPECIES_____( )   SPECIES_____( )

SPECIES_____( )   SPECIES_____( )

BEST FLY_____

ADDITIONAL NOTES_____

_____

LOCATION_____DATE_____

DIRECTIONS_____

_____

_____

WATER LEVEL_____

ROD_____

TECHNIQUE:_____DRY_____NYMPH_____STREAMER

SPECIES_____( )   SPECIES_____( )

SPECIES_____( )   SPECIES_____( )

BEST FLY_____

ADDITIONAL NOTES_____

_____

LOCATION_____DATE_____

DIRECTIONS_____

_____

_____

WATER LEVEL_____

ROD_____

TECHNIQUE:_____DRY_____NYMPH_____STREAMER

SPECIES_____( )   SPECIES_____( )

SPECIES_____( )   SPECIES_____( )

BEST FLY_____

ADDITIONAL NOTES_____

_____

LOCATION_____DATE_____

DIRECTIONS_____

_____

_____

WATER LEVEL_____

ROD_____

TECHNIQUE:_____DRY_____NYMPH_____STREAMER

SPECIES_____( )   SPECIES_____( )

SPECIES_____( )   SPECIES_____( )

BEST FLY_____

ADDITIONAL NOTES_____

_____

LOCATION_____DATE_____

DIRECTIONS_____

_____

_____

WATER LEVEL_____

ROD_____

TECHNIQUE:_____DRY_____NYMPH_____STREAMER

SPECIES_____( )   SPECIES_____( )

SPECIES_____( )   SPECIES_____( )

BEST FLY_____

ADDITIONAL NOTES_____

_____

LOCATION_____DATE_____

DIRECTIONS_____

_____

_____

WATER LEVEL_____

ROD_____

TECHNIQUE:_____DRY_____NYMPH_____STREAMER

SPECIES_____( )   SPECIES_____( )

SPECIES_____( )   SPECIES_____( )

BEST FLY_____

ADDITIONAL NOTES_____

_____

LOCATION_____DATE_____

DIRECTIONS_____

_____

_____

WATER LEVEL_____

ROD_____

TECHNIQUE:_____DRY_____NYMPH_____STREAMER

SPECIES_____( ) SPECIES_____( )

SPECIES_____( ) SPECIES_____( )

BEST FLY_____

ADDITIONAL NOTES_____

_____

LOCATION_____DATE_____

DIRECTIONS_____

_____

_____

WATER LEVEL_____

ROD_____

TECHNIQUE:_____DRY_____NYMPH_____STREAMER

SPECIES_____( ) SPECIES_____( )

SPECIES_____( ) SPECIES_____( )

BEST FLY_____

ADDITIONAL NOTES_____

_____

LOCATION_____DATE_____

DIRECTIONS_____

_____

_____

WATER LEVEL_____

ROD_____

TECHNIQUE:_____DRY_____NYMPH_____STREAMER

SPECIES_____( )   SPECIES_____( )

SPECIES_____( )   SPECIES_____( )

BEST FLY_____

ADDITIONAL NOTES_____

_____

LOCATION_____DATE_____

DIRECTIONS_____

_____

_____

WATER LEVEL_____

ROD_____

TECHNIQUE:_____DRY_____NYMPH_____STREAMER

SPECIES_____( )   SPECIES_____( )

SPECIES_____( )   SPECIES_____( )

BEST FLY_____

ADDITIONAL NOTES_____

_____

LOCATION_____DATE_____
DIRECTIONS_____
_____
_____
WATER LEVEL_____
ROD_____
TECHNIQUE:_____DRY_____NYMPH_____STREAMER
SPECIES_____( ) SPECIES_____( )
SPECIES_____( ) SPECIES_____( )
BEST FLY_____
ADDITIONAL NOTES_____
_____

LOCATION_____DATE_____
DIRECTIONS_____
_____
_____
WATER LEVEL_____
ROD_____
TECHNIQUE:_____DRY_____NYMPH_____STREAMER
SPECIES_____( ) SPECIES_____( )
SPECIES_____( ) SPECIES_____( )
BEST FLY_____
ADDITIONAL NOTES_____
_____

Made in the USA
Las Vegas, NV
27 May 2022